HOW TO HAVE A
HAPPY BIRTHDAY

Praise For

HOW TO HAVE A HAPPY BIRTHDAY

"Filled with wise insight that inspires and motivates readers to thoughtfully create their birthday celebration with as much good energy as possible, this book is an invitation to experience the transformative joy a birthday can provide. Tamar Hurwitz-Fleming's voice rings true with kindness, compassion, and unique birthday sparkle."

—RAE DUNN, artist and author of *In Pursuit of Inspiration*

"Tamar Hurwitz-Fleming has masterfully crafted a direct answer for those of us who have ever questioned our self-love, worthiness, or personal power. This book is for everyone who is willing to explore how we celebrate our birthday as an entry point to our mental health and social wellness. With spiritually wise instruction, Hurwitz-Fleming guides us through story-telling, deep observation, and self-assessment into an interactive experience that supports our ability to design more than a happy birthday—it's truly an integrative holistic approach to designing a healthier life."

—MARIANNA SOUSA, social wellness leader

"There are countless books and articles on the significance of all major holidays, with one glaring exception: our birthdays. *How to Have a Happy Birthday* makes a potent case for not only why birthdays matter but also how to celebrate them in ways that enhance the human experience. All of our lives are singular and sacred, and centering our birthdays is indeed a spiritual act. Finally, there is a book I can recommend to my clients who struggle with their birthdays."

—DEBORAH COOPER, MA, MFT, marriage & family therapist

"Birthdays can be wonderful expressions of our unique time on earth but are often fraught with disappointment and missed opportunities. This book is a soothing balm, and the guidance offered is tender and robust. Hurwitz-Fleming uses personal anecdotes as well as teaching stories to illustrate her birthday wisdom—everything from the mundane to deeply powerful spiritual truths. She endows the reader with all that is needed to take charge of our birthdays and create the joy that is possible in them. If you've ever wished you'd had a happier birthday, this book is for you."

—ALICIA ELKORT, author of *A Map of Every Undoing*

HOW TO HAVE A
HAPPY BIRTHDAY

Create Meaning, Fulfillment,
and Joy on Your Special Day

TAMAR HURWITZ-FLEMING

Date Palm Books

The information contained in this book is based on the author's personal experiences and opinions and from others she interviewed during many years. The publisher and author are not responsible for any adverse effects or consequences resulting from the use of the suggestions discussed in this book. Should the reader have any questions concerning the appropriateness of any suggestions mentioned, the author and publisher strongly suggest consulting with a professional psychologist, therapist, or spiritual adviser.

All the stories in this book are true. The names have been changed to protect the privacy of the individuals involved.

Illustrations by Tamar Hurwitz-Fleming
Author photo on page 130 by Rina Eliashar
Cover design by Laura Duffy
Book design by Karen Minster

Thanks to Gay Hendricks, PhD, and Kathlyn Hendricks, PhD, for allowing the author to reprint from their book, *Conscious Loving: The Journey to Co-Commitment.*

Published by Date Palm Books, Sarasota, FL, DatePalmBooks.com

For bulk purchase inquiries: info@DatePalmBooks.com

For media and speaking inquiries and to contact the author:
Birthday@TamarHF.com

979-8-9884606-0-2   (paperback)
979-8-9884606-1-9   (hardcover)
979-8-9884606-3-3   (ebook)
979-8-9884606-4-0   (audiobook)

Library of Congress Control Number: 2023916550

In loving memory
of my cherished parents,
Rina and Joe.

A portion of the proceeds
from the sale of this book will be
donated to muttville.org
and other nonprofit organizations
supporting animal rescue.

CONTENTS

INTRODUCTION

3

1. THE MOST IMPORTANT DAY OF THE YEAR
Why Birthdays Matter

5

2. THE MOST CHALLENGING DAY OF THE YEAR
Transform the Birthday Blues

17

3. CREATE THE DAY
How to Prepare for Your Birthday

31

4. CELEBRATE THE DAY
Put Yourself at the Center

49

5. WHAT NOT TO DO ON YOUR BIRTHDAY
Support Your Chances for a Happy Day

63

6. YOUR BIRTHDAY AND THE HOLIDAYS
Keep Yourself at the Center

73

7. CELEBRATE OTHERS
Add Sparkle to the Birthday Spirit

79

8. CELEBRATE WITH SERIOUS ILLNESS
A Poignant Time to Share Love

87

A FINAL WORD:
Birthdays Can Be So Happy

91

HOW TO PLAN YOUR HAPPY BIRTHDAY
A Workbook for Insight, Inspiration, and Ideas

93

Acknowledgments
127

About the Author
131

Author's Note
133

HOW TO HAVE A
HAPPY
BIRTHDAY

INTRODUCTION

Birthdays can be magnificent. Whether they are adventurous, solitary, social, romantic, or family oriented, birthdays invite us to revel in love's spotlight once a year. If we are willing to absorb positive energy when it's our time to celebrate, we can be infused with a happiness that nourishes our soul. For many of us, this can be difficult.

Can you recall your first birthday memory? Mine was when I was three. I can still remember the taste of the chocolate cake roll with whipped cream and pastel confetti sprinkles, and the confusion of my emotions. In the years that followed, I had a string of somewhat happy, sad, and terrible birthdays until I turned twenty and realized that, if I wanted to have a satisfying birthday, I needed to take responsibility for creating my own magic. After all, it was my birthday—nobody else's. And to ensure it hit the highest note, I understood that I needed to be the architect of my own birthday experience.

Everybody has a birthday, and it is equally defined by a twenty-four-hour period. It's one of the few facts every human being has exactly in common. When we celebrate our birthday with presence, not just presents, the experience can be delightful and profound.

I wrote this book to offer uplifting reasons and practical advice to support everyone having a wonderful birthday!

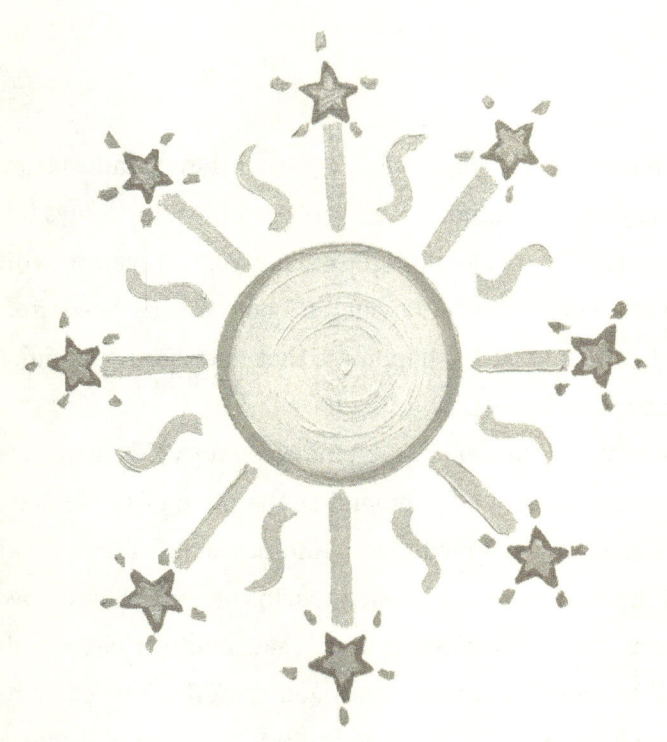

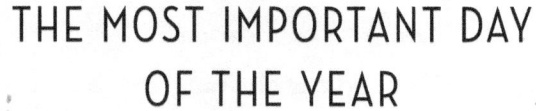

THE MOST IMPORTANT DAY OF THE YEAR

Why Birthdays Matter

Your birthday is a major holiday. Though banks won't close and fireworks displays won't be lit in your honor, it's the most meaningful holiday you can celebrate. That's because your birthday is the one day to officially celebrate you. Why does that matter? Because your life matters. Because you matter.

When I turned eighteen, I had my worst birthday. It was my freshman year at the University of California, Santa Cruz, and I was living in the dorms. I woke up expecting the phone to ring with cheerful greetings from my family, but the phone was silent. I went to my classes, after which I rushed back to my room to spend the rest of the afternoon waiting. (This was before cell phones.)

"Maybe they are having a busy day," I reasoned. By dinnertime I was glum. I was perplexed that my family hadn't called. "They must be planning to phone me at night." So I hurried back from dinner to sit by the phone, yet no phone calls came.

By the time I went to bed at 11:30 p.m., I was stunned. I was the baby of the family, it was my first year away from home, and I was celebrating a momentous birthday. How could my family forget me? I was so sad that I buried myself under the covers so I could muffle the sound of my sobbing. I didn't want my roommate to hear me.

Finally, at 11:50 p.m. the phone rang. It was my best friend, Tracy, who was spending the year in Germany. She was broke but had scraped up some coins to call me from a pay phone for two minutes. I started crying again when I recounted that my family had forgotten my birthday. Her compassion, devotion, and friendship were a powerful balm to my heartbreak. I was so grateful that someone loved me enough to remember my birthday and make the effort to reach out.

A day later, the phone calls started. Everyone had a reason explaining why they didn't call on my birthday—and a sincere apology for forgetting—but even if they did feel bad, the damage was done. Indeed, since birthdays have a profound way of magnifying our insecurities, this symbolic moment validated what I'd always believed about myself: I didn't matter and I wasn't loved.

Two years later, I was living in Poitiers, France, during my junior year abroad. I was turning twenty—a big milestone— and I ended up having the best birthday of my life. I woke up realizing my day was all up to me. Perhaps it was because I had newfound independence living by myself. Perhaps it was because I was living abroad, having an exhilarating experience. Perhaps it was because I wasn't going to rely on others anymore to impact the quality of my birthday.

Whatever the reason, I took the day off from classes and ended up meandering through town with a light step and a big smile, and I splurged on a fancy bottle of French perfume that I'd been coveting. Although it was expensive and I'd have to struggle that month on my meager student budget, I gave myself permission to buy a birthday present— something I'd never done before, but had always waited for others to do for me.

That night, I gathered some friends together to mark the occasion with a festive dinner at my apartment. Everyone welcomed a reason to celebrate; we were all far from home and appreciated any excuse to socialize. My friends showed up with sincere joy for me, and some came with little gifts and cards.

We had a wonderful time, and after that day—the day I finally took control of how I wanted to celebrate me—I realized that the secret to having a happy birthday was to make it be the way I wanted. To not depend on others to do it for me, and certainly not to sit passively waiting for the phone to ring.

FIND YOUR JOY

Celebrating your birthday intentionally helps you take responsibility for your joy. Putting yourself first and planning what you truly want gives you the experience and positive results that come from making the choice to do what makes you happy. Some of us don't even know what we want. Use your birthday as a way to tune into your essential nature and discover what brings you unfettered joy.

HONOR THE SOUL

Why are birthdays meaningful? There are many reasons, but to get to the heart of it, we have to get spiritual for a moment. Let's go deep. Let's start with your birth. Along with death, it's the most powerful moment of your life. When you took your first breath, your spirit fully entered your newborn body and marked the beginning of your current life. As such, the moment of our birth, when our souls take physical form, is the ultimate marriage vow. It's spirit and body, hand in hand, 'til death do we part.

This is why our birthday is the most deeply personal day of the year. It is the day we are most aligned with our soul. It is the day we are most spiritually porous and therefore able to receive an abundance of positive energy if we allow it in. Since we all need—and get to have—the love and spiritual connection that is available to us on our birthday, it's important to pay homage to the day. Birthdays offer us one day a year to press the pause button on the rest of our life and celebrate our humanity and our reason for being.

CELEBRATE EVERYONE, EVERYWHERE

The good news is that birthdays are an equal opportunity provider. They offer the same spiritual riches to everyone on the planet no matter who we are, how we live, or what cultures we belong to. Everyone has a birthday, and everyone has the right to celebrate it. Celebrating is a form of ritual that commemorates something significant. Though typically thought of as fun occasions with friends, family, and gifts, celebrations can also be thoughtful and deeply meaningful.

Either way, by embracing our birthday celebration, we choose an opportunity that can provide mindful centering and self-love. In turn, this can help us heal emotional wounds and soften to the world around us.

Self-love shouldn't be confused with narcissism or selfishness. On the contrary, it's your gentle awareness of self-acceptance and compassion. And the natural result that comes with self-love is increased kindness and love for others. The old adage is true: We can't love others more than we can love ourselves. The times you've felt the most loving toward someone are directly related to the times you've felt the softest inside yourself. It's a beautiful feeling, and though it's often elusive, self-love is worth nurturing whenever possible.

RECEIVE THE LOVE

Have you ever noticed how people are happy when it's your birthday? If not, start noticing. Go tell the barista behind the counter, "It's my birthday today!" and watch them light up. There's a natural understanding that when it's your day, you're special.

Because we all know our own birthday will come around to offer the uplifting treasures of the day, we are inspired to feel happy for others. It's like being in a circle on the dance floor when someone goes into the middle to boogie solo and be the momentary star. Everyone enthusiastically cheers them on because it's fun and because they know they'll eventually get their turn in the center and be exalted too.

While hamming it up on the dance floor and soaking up the cheers can be easy to do, receiving love in our daily life isn't always so easy to do. One way to practice this is to shift into gratitude and say *thank you* when it comes your way. Whether someone is giving you a compliment, wishing you all the best, or beaming smiles of happiness at you, putting all your defenses, excuses, and discomfort on hold for a moment to simply say *thank you* helps you receive the positive energy directed at you. It helps you receive the love.

Since birthdays happen only one day a year, they contain a safety release valve so that you don't get overwhelmed with "too much love." Too much love? Who doesn't want all the love they can get? Pay close attention.

In their insightful book, *Conscious Loving: The Journey to Co-Commitment*, therapists Gay and Kathlyn Hendricks introduce the concept of what they call the Upper Limits Problem. Simply defined, the Upper Limits Problem occurs when "we cannot feel good for very long without invoking some negative experience to bring us down."

The authors explain that "due to our past conditioning, we all have a limit on how much positive energy we can tolerate. Go past this limit and an alarm bell goes off in our unconscious mind." They believe that learning "how to feel good naturally, without chemical assistance, is a new task in evolution." Our job? "To allow ourselves to open additional positive-energy channels."

Since birthdays are only one day a year, they provide a perfect opportunity to practice integrating more positive energy into our lives. Birthdays confront the Upper Limits Problem head on, because who can argue with feeling good one day a year? Indeed, our birthdays are the one day we can absolutely indulge ourselves with the happy abandon that comes from a playful heart opened wide to receive joy without restraint. It's just like boogying in the center of the dance floor.

ACCEPT YOUR AGE

Another reason to consciously celebrate your birthday is that it ritualizes the passing of time. Granted, in certain cultures, especially in externally driven, consumer-dominated ones like the United States, "getting old" is often portrayed as a failure. We're encouraged to lie about our age, make self-deprecating jokes about being "over the hill," and inflict judgment and shame on others or ourselves just because we're getting older. However, in those cultures that still place family in the center—especially those that have three generations living at home—elders typically enjoy revered status, as they should.

For those of us who have lived long enough, we value the perspective, wisdom, and confidence that time bestows, not to mention the good fortune of having another year of life. Therefore, accepting and celebrating our age becomes a source of authentic gratitude and power.

In this book, I present some real stories about real people whose names I've changed for privacy.

LIKE MOTHER, LIKE DAUGHTER

Joan was a beautiful woman who was committed to remaining that way as she grew older. Because Joan was raised to believe that being old implied you were less beautiful (and therefore less powerful) than being young, Joan never admitted her age, even to her children. She also refused to acknowledge or celebrate her birthday because she didn't want to call attention to being another year older.

As a result, her daughter Allison subconsciously internalized Joan's approach to birthdays. Even though Allison willingly admitted her age and celebrated her husband's and children's birthdays with creativity and good cheer, she never fully celebrated her own. It wasn't until she turned forty-three and had a conversation with a close friend that she realized this inherited mindset had kept her own birthday rituals subdued.

That year Allison chose to create the birthday she wanted. It was an uplifting, fun, and healing experience that helped her step more fully into her power, especially as an aging woman herself.

Every age has its beauty. Notice people older than you who radiate inner beauty and confidence and still maintain their personal style. See them as your role models. And try to become that role model for others. Know that by embracing your age, you are changing reality for the better and modeling excellent behavior. Liberate yourself and enjoy it.

RITUALIZE THE PASSAGE OF TIME

Ritualizing age is an ancient tradition. Whether it's the thirteen-year-old Bar or Bat Mitzvah in Judaism, the Fiesta de Quinceañera in Latin American culture, or the secular Sweet Sixteen in the United States, our teenage years coincide with puberty and represent a shift from childhood to young adulthood. Creating age rituals for this time of life makes sense, and many cultures around the world currently and historically enacted these rituals. Here in the United States, other rituals around aging tend to happen when we turn eighteen, twenty-one, and all the other five-year and ten-year milestones like thirty-five and forty.

It's important to annually acknowledge our age through birthday rituals because it reminds us that time is passing. And time, as we know it, is a nonrenewable resource. As disheartening as that may be to some, ignoring this reality makes it more likely that we squander our lives without accomplishing or experiencing what we most value. When you realize the clock really is ticking, it can be the wake-up call that snaps you into action. What is it you really want to do with your life? It feels different looking at it from the age of forty-nine than from the age of twenty-three.

MAKE THE DREAM COME TRUE

Evan was a successful businessman who ran his own company in Los Angeles. A fun-loving guy his whole life, Evan brought humor to daily situations and loved planning exciting activities and surprises for his family.

As his fiftieth birthday approached that summer, he wanted to celebrate this milestone in a bold way. The world was his oyster and there were no limits. Should he take a backcountry journey up the Amazon? Spend time at the base camp of Mt. Everest? Rent a luxury bus and follow the Grateful Dead on tour? After months of soul-searching about what would bring him the most joy and satisfaction to celebrate this momentous birthday, he finally realized what he wanted to do. He wanted to go back to summer camp.

Ever since he was a child, Evan had spent the happiest days of his life at a rustic boys' camp in New England, and he even became a camp counselor there in his teens. He sent his sons to the same camp and dreamed of opening his own summer camp one day. He excitedly contacted the camp's owners and made his offer: if they put him up and fed him, he'd go to work and help them in whatever way they needed. They jumped at the opportunity.

So, that summer, Evan spent a blissful month unplugged from all the responsibilities and concerns of his daily life back home. Whether he was helping off-load boxes of potatoes for dinner, mowing the vast lawn in the sticky heat, or supervising the campers during outdoor activities, Evan hadn't felt as carefree and happy in decades.

That experience began an annual tradition where he continues to return to camp every summer to help out. He decided there was no need to start his own camp anymore if he could go back there, and he ended up buying a home nearby. Turning fifty gave Evan the excuse to "dream big," and it has since allowed him to literally make his dream come true.

It's also important to ritualize our birthdays and the passing of time because rituals give structure to change. By making the choice to honor your age, you create an opportunity to adjust to the change your age represents—however you define it for yourself. Face it, ritualize it, and integrate the experience so that the years don't fly by and eventually catch you by surprise when you wake up one day and you're sixty-seven and you wonder, "How the heck did that happen?"

2

THE MOST CHALLENGING DAY OF THE YEAR

Transform the Birthday Blues

Birthdays are supposed to be happy, yet they can often be disappointing. Melancholy will arise just before our birthday that conceals a yearning for something that is unarticulated, or otherwise unresolved. Since birthdays symbolize our most spiritually aligned day, our yearning tends to be for deeper personal meaning, whether we are aware of it or not.

Many of us were raised in households that didn't adequately support our sensitive souls. As a result, we got programmed early to invoke negative experiences if we find ourselves feeling good for any length of time. This negativity conveniently loves to make an appearance right around our birthdays. Sprinkle in some melancholy and, voilà, we have the perfect recipe for sabotaging our special day.

We undermine our birthdays because we have such a big need around them. It's our own major holiday, right? Rather than risk disappointment, many of us prefer to remain numb to the potential of our big day. We create defenses and justifications to keep the energy of our birthday dim. Simply put: We suppress or sabotage our birthday because we believe, even unwittingly, that it protects us to do so.

A CHARLIE BROWN BIRTHDAY

Vanessa was an only child whose father was a high-powered corporate lawyer and whose mother busied herself with charitable causes. Vanessa's parents were rarely home at night due to a brimming social schedule, and the night of her fourteenth birthday, they were going to a black-tie event. It was family tradition to present a birthday cake on everyone's actual birthday, and Vanessa waited expectantly for that to happen.

Her parents were running late that evening and eventually took a moment from getting ready to bring her the cake. Her mother hadn't finished dressing for the party, and she brought out the cake wearing her bathrobe as she and Vanessa's father started singing "Happy birthday to you—"

Moments after they began, the phone rang. Without hesitating, Vanessa's father broke away to answer. His clients called at all hours, and he always put them first. "It's business," he'd say, as if that explained why family came second. During this brief and special moment for Vanessa, his choice wasn't any different. She still came second.

So her mother continued singing to her alone, "Happy birthday to you ... happy birrrrth—" And what happened next is hard to believe but true: Vanessa's mother couldn't finish the song. She was so deter-mined to be on time for the party that she ran off impatiently, saying she needed to finish dressing and do her makeup.

There Vanessa stood. Alone. And she finished singing to herself, barely choking out the words: "Happy birthday, dear Vanessa, happy birthday to you." She was heartbroken, and that experience sub-consciously formed a belief that she wasn't worthy of even the simplest of celebrations.

NINE WAYS WE (OR OTHERS) SABOTAGE OUR BIRTHDAYS

1. Ignoring Birthdays

One way we sabotage our birthday is by ignoring them. We convincingly tell ourselves and others, "My birthday isn't a big deal," or "My birthday is just another day." We believe these ideas so we don't have to confront the power and potential pain. It's much easier to ignore a birthday and let it pass with a wistful sigh of relief than it is to become vulnerable to our deeper needs and desires, and confess that, really, we do want to feel special on that day.

Since we secretly (or overtly) believe that no one cares about our birthday, we adopt a "Why bother?" attitude as a way to proactively defend against the disappointment we inevitably feel. Even if someone does care, it's often too little, too late. And frankly, since it's our own personal holiday, it doesn't matter if fifty people are lined up singing to us—it doesn't kick in unless we own, fully participate in, and help create the experience of the day. Our day.

RESCUE ME

When Mika turned seventeen, she didn't have any birthday plans. She was a sensitive teenager without much self-esteem and didn't invite her friends to do anything. Her birthday fell on a Sunday that year and she stayed home to watch football. She opened up a big bag of potato chips and ate the whole thing during the first quarter.

When her friend Ron called around noon, he was surprised to hear that Mika didn't have any celebratory plans, so he enthusiastically invited her to do something. Unfortunately, Mika had already settled into a "Why bother?" attitude and couldn't be convinced to join Ron for some birthday fun, even if it was something simple like getting frozen yogurt.

Ron tried hard to change Mika's mind but couldn't succeed, even though, secretly inside, Mika did want to feel special and celebrate her day. She wanted Ron to insist on celebrating with her. She wanted Ron to come over anyway and make her go out for fun. She wanted Ron to do everything in his power to rescue her from her own pool of self-pity.

Unfortunately, Mika's secret wish did not come true. Ron tried his best, but had to respect Mika's choice, and when they hung up the phone, Mika started crying. The only party she attended that day was her own pity party.

---

2. Getting Depressed

Along with the melancholy that can tarnish our birthday experience, so can depression. While those two feelings are related, they are distinctly different. One (melancholy) reveals a hunger for something deeper, while the other (depression) flattens us with hopelessness and despair. Typically, we get melancholic or depressed before our birthdays because, in the past, we have felt disappointed by them, and therefore shut ourselves down. This feedback loop perpetuates the negative cycle.

Our spirits might drop before our birthday for many reasons. Perhaps we feel time passing too quickly while realizing we haven't been fulfilling our potential. Or maybe we've bought into the falsehood that "aging makes us less valuable." If you find that you feel depressed on your birthday, or in the weeks before, start tuning in to the reasons your feelings are being triggered and try to bring some awareness to the surface. By doing this, you can confront the causes head on and possibly have a breakthrough moment where the illusion shatters and the radiant light pours through—even if it starts with just a glimmering twinkle.

3. Keeping Your Birthday a Secret

Another way we sabotage our birthday is that we keep it a secret. We don't remind our friends and we don't inform our colleagues because we don't want to appear self-centered.

Perhaps we had working parents, social parents, creative parents, alcoholic parents, or narcissistic parents who prioritized those things in their life over giving us enough attention as children. As such, we might believe that no one really wants to take the time for us. Sound familiar? If so, consider yourself one among millions.

And count yourself lucky that you're now able to make sense of those odd, conflicting feelings that start emerging around your birthday, because if you understand them, you can change them. By informing others that it's your birthday, you allow them to generate positive energy for you. It's something they sincerely want to do!

4. Not Planning

Another way we sabotage our birthday is by not giving people advance notice so they can prepare to celebrate. If you wait until the day before your birthday to ask your friends to party with you, they may be unavailable. Same thing with your colleagues. If you tell them at the end of the workday that it's your birthday, they likely won't be able to run out and get you a cake or have drinks with you after work.

While it appears you're being spontaneous (which tends to be a trait held in high regard), it conveniently prevents others from being able to celebrate you. Last-minute announcements may also be hard on your friends who may feel stressed, disappointed, or guilty that they were caught off guard and were unprepared to celebrate your birthday.

5. Having Childlike Expectations

There is a flip side to believing that no one wants to take the time to celebrate our birthday. Instead, we might have an unconscious expectation that others should do all the work to make our birthday happy. If our parents celebrated our birthdays when we were kids, they may have made us feel loved with presents and birthday parties. They did it all, and we grew to expect this every year.

However, somewhere along the way, most of our parents stopped creating our birthday ritual for us, especially once we became teens or moved out of the house. Suddenly, what was once a magical, enchanting day full of promise became a regular disappointment because our parents weren't in charge anymore.

Most of us do not realize the powerful impact of this shift, so we project this parental role onto other people in our life—our friends, our roommates, our significant other. We subconsciously expect them to proactively feel the joy and do the work for us like our parents did. This can often lead to disappointment and even anger, which is another way we sabotage our birthday.

THE LITTLE PRINCE

A few days before he turned twenty-eight, Robert was talking with a colleague when the subject of his birthday randomly came up. The big day fell on a Friday that year, and when his colleague asked what he was planning to do, Robert's energy noticeably dropped as he replied that he might go out for drinks with friends after work.

His perceptive colleague who was "Birthday Positive" dug a little deeper. He could tell Robert seemed a bit anxious about his approaching birthday and wanted to know why. Eventually Robert revealed that when he was a kid growing up, his mother always made a big deal about birthdays. She was really into them, planned them down to the tiniest detail, and always made Robert feel like a prince.

Ever since he left home, Robert's mother wasn't there to orchestrate his birthday celebrations, and they never had the same magic. So Robert let his birthdays languish, believing that happy birthdays only belonged to the realm of childhood.

After a wholehearted pep talk from his colleague, Robert realized he'd been held back by his childhood experiences and was excited that he had the power now to create his own birthday joy.

Since your birthday, by definition, is most significant to you, you need to put most of your energy into it, even if it's to ask for and genuinely receive the efforts of others. That way, you take full responsibility for the joy of your birthday and free up the heavy expectations that can weigh you down.

You might have the best partner or friend who produces enchanting razzle-dazzle for you every year, yet because you're stuck in negative beliefs about your birthday, you're locked in the "nothing is good enough" doom loop and become impossible to please. Like a stubborn child desperate for attention, you dig in your heels and keep these painful belief systems rooted in place.

6. Others Don't Want to Celebrate Us

Sometimes, people closest to us aren't as into our birthdays as we'd like or expect them to be. Perhaps they feel so deficient and malnourished themselves in that department that they can't find any joyous energy for us. Or maybe they have resentment toward us that is buried deeply (or not so deeply) and they refuse to celebrate us when they still carry the burden of their own unresolved pain.

Birthdays are kind of a litmus test within relationships. If a partner is aloof and uninterested in showing up for our day, especially if we've been asking them to, chances are high that there's some meaningful work on themselves or on the relationship that needs to be done.

On the flip side, when you're taking charge of your birthday celebration, be sure to include your significant other at the beginning of your birthday planning so they don't feel excluded, because that can generate pain in the relationship as well.

7. Getting Sick

Another way we might sabotage our birthday is by getting sick. Many factors can weaken our immune system including lack of sleep, poor diet, too much alcohol, too much anger, and the granddaddy of them all: stress. Since birthdays can be stressful, it's easy to understand how just when our birthdays show up, we magically get sick. Many of us would rather face illness than the pressure or disappointment of our birthday. It can be a convenient (if physically uncomfortable) way to avoid taking responsibility for making our day happy.

We don't need to be hard on ourselves if we get sick on our birthday. Instead, we can value the natural release and introspection illness brings, and use the altered feeling that comes with it to relax deeper into our birthday experience.

Be gentle with yourself if you're sick. Just go with the flow and let yourself absorb the healing birthday energy. Birthdays still deserve our presence and can still be rich, even if we're temporarily sick. I know, because this happened to me on a big birthday.

In 2016, I celebrated my fiftieth birthday. January 9 fell on a Saturday that year, which was a lucky fact I had known for at least a decade. For years I dreamed of a big celebration. This was particularly true because I'd never been married and always craved a noteworthy party like those typically associated with weddings. So, over the years I'd randomly announce to those in my circle, "When I turn fifty, it's going to fall on a Saturday night and I'm going to rent a hall, have it catered, hire a DJ with a disco ball, and invite all my friends to celebrate with me!"

Four months before my fiftieth birthday, I got engaged. Suddenly, planning a huge birthday party made no sense since my fiancé and I were going to throw a big wedding party nine months later. I had to change my plans. Instead, I had a small birthday party at home, which included some close friends and my entire family flying in to celebrate with me, some even showing up as a surprise. It was a sweet and lovely party that everyone really enjoyed.

Unfortunately, I got sick during the days leading up to my celebration. I'd returned from an overseas trip a week earlier, was grappling with jet lag, and caught a cold. I'd also put a lot of pressure on myself to have the best fiftieth birthday party ever, and that pressure needed a release. Getting sick did the trick.

Fortunately, by the time my birthday rolled around, the worst of it was over, and I was able to be as present as possible. But in the days leading up to my birthday, my light was dim and I was unable to summon any joyous pre-birthday anticipation. Worse, I worried I would have to cancel my party and be sick in bed on my big day.

The good news? Despite the lead-up to my big birthday being thwarted, I didn't get down on myself about it. I just accepted my cold for what it was and realized that I'd put way too much pressure on myself (ten years' worth!) in my birthday planning. I chose to let go of all my expectations and just show up. And in the end, I had a memorable and happy birthday celebration.

8. Generating Distress

Because we are extra sensitive as our birthday approaches, we can sometimes feel irritated or act insensitively toward others, including the people who are closest to us. This in turn can end up causing distress and generate difficult interactions that bring our energy down just in time for our special day.

If you notice tensions rising before your birthday, or those closest to you point out that something is "off" in your countenance, then consider it a sign to turn inward and give yourself an honest assessment. Ask why you're feeling sad or afraid as your birthday approaches, and chances are you'll readily find the answer. Use that information to create what you want for your birthday and watch your energy shift. You may need to cry first, but the glimmers of light are there to sparkle brightly if you're willing to generate enough self-empathy.

9. Letting the Past Dominate the Present

Sometimes our birthdays coincide with difficult, traumatic, or heartbreaking experiences or events that get replayed in our psyche on our special day. While most unfortunate, we still have the right to allow ourselves to enjoy our birthdays despite the painful memories.

If you're in this situation and feel unable to release yourself from the upsetting past, you might want to consider pursuing forms of safe and effective therapy like EMDR, which can help lessen the traumatic memories so you can fully embrace the specialness of your birthday.

THE POWER IS YOURS

Although there are many other ways we can sabotage our birthdays and bring on the birthday blues, the most pressing thing to be conscious of is that many of us choose to do this to ourselves. We are not victims.

By becoming aware of this pattern, and the reasons behind it, we can elect to make a different choice. We can compassionately say hello to the fears and disappointments and let them have some breathing room while drawing a boundary like a firm, loving parent and saying, "No more. I will not let you ruin my birthdays anymore. I deserve to be happy. I deserve to receive love. And I deserve to celebrate my own major holiday."

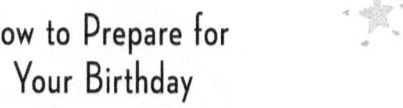

3

CREATE THE DAY

How to Prepare for Your Birthday

PLAN FOR A BIG HOLIDAY!

Now that you're ready to fully celebrate, how do you prepare? Well, just like any momentous holiday, preparing for your birthday is an ongoing process that you should start thinking about one month in advance. By doing so, you begin welcoming the spirit of the season and it gives you enough time to consider options that may require extra planning, unless it's a big milestone birthday that requires planning at least a year ahead if you want to do something big, like take an exotic trip.

A ONCE-IN-A-LIFETIME CELEBRATION

Lee was always enthusiastic about her birthdays. When it came time for her sixtieth birthday, Lee went for it. Just after turning fifty-nine, she sat down with her wife, Ari, and said, "I want to go on a big trip to Europe to celebrate. I also want to party with friends at home." Since Lee loved barbecue and Ping-Pong, they planned for this on her actual birthday, which guaranteed pure joy. She asked her wife and daughter to make her favorite birthday cake and requested that her brother work the grill so they wouldn't have to hire someone. That way they could save for their European extravaganza. They saved up throughout the year, putting money away each month.

They went away for three weeks the following spring, one of those weeks being a writing retreat for Lee alone in her favorite city of Amsterdam. The other two weeks were spent with her wife and daughter visiting places she'd never seen. And every single place they went on the trip, Lee would announce, "This is my sixtieth birthday trip!" which resulted in about twenty extra pieces of birthday cake and candles throughout the long—and satisfying—milestone celebration.

PONDER THE MEANING

Like all holidays, there is a deeper meaning to your birthday and the coming year. What might it be?

Does it relate to your age and how it culturally or personally signifies some sort of milestone? Does it relate to worthwhile work you feel called to do or create in the future? Does it pertain to letting go of entrenched ideas about what your life is "supposed to be like" versus what it actually is? Or is it just a gentle, yet powerful reminder that yet another year has passed and it's up to you to grab your life by the horns and live the life you truly want to live?

Even if you're not ready to sell everything and go live on a sailboat for the rest of your years, consider what you need to do to achieve that ultimate and possible dream. Or at least get more comfortable with the life you have.

GET AN ASTROLOGY OR TAROT READING

If you would like spiritual guidance for the coming year, consider getting an astrology or tarot reading in the days leading up to your birthday. If this intrigues you, ask people you trust if they know of anyone to recommend. Don't take this lightly. Opening ourselves to others who talk about our lives in profound ways is a powerful, yet vulnerable act. Don't abdicate your power or your inner truth to anyone, and only absorb the information that feels right. Discern for yourself, and then let the spiritual messages that come through uplift and support your journey for the coming year.

THE POWER OF SUGGESTION

When Flora turned twenty-two, she wanted to celebrate by getting a psychic reading. She never had one before and was excited to have someone "predict her future," so she set up an appointment with a woman who came recommended.

While most of the reading seemed to resonate with Flora, she was surprised to hear the psychic tell her that she would get a job at a nursing home. Flora couldn't think of anything less appropriate for her. She loved elderly people, but she was not cut out to be a caregiver and felt depressed at the thought. Flora really just wanted to work in a coffee shop.

Nevertheless, in the weeks that followed, Flora looked for jobs in a variety of nursing homes because that's what the psychic said. Fortunately, no one got back to her. One day, as she passed by a neighborhood café, she saw a "help wanted" sign in the window. She walked in and was immediately hired. She felt so relieved that she didn't have to work in a nursing home.

It was only later that Flora realized she was abdicating her own power in order to fulfill the psychic's prophecy. It was a valuable insight she learned at a young age.

CLEAR CLUTTER

Since your birthday is your own personal new year, use it as an opportunity to clear out old, stagnant energy. This includes material items, emotional/psychological baggage, spiritual blocks, and relationship issues.

Start a month before so that you have a limited time to focus on this task (otherwise it can be too overwhelming) and yet enough time to be effective. By making good effort to clear clutter, you'll feel a sense of accomplishment and buoyancy when your birthday finally arrives.

CREATE A BIRTHDAY ALTAR

Much the same way we decorate and create festive spaces for holidays, create a similar space for your birthday. Find a place in your home to adorn with favorite photos from childhood and birthdays past. You might also want to include photos of your parents, ancestors, friends, and pets. Add fresh flowers, colorful candles, pretty rocks, sparkling crystals, and anything else that inspires you. Do this at least one week in advance of your birthday, if not sooner.

It's also powerful to create a birthday altar on your birthday eve as a way to prepare for the specialness of the following day. By creating a birthday altar, you invoke the magic that welcomes a vibrant and celebratory birthday spirit. At the end of your birthday, pack up any items you'd like to keep for future birthday altars and add items to the box throughout the year if anything shows up in your life that has meaning.

ENVISION WHAT YOU WANT

Since your birthday is so spiritually infused, use its magical effect to consider what you'd like to invite into your coming year. Would you like to be more creative? If so, what form does that creativity take? How do you see yourself taking creative action? Where? When? Do you welcome more abundance into your life? If so, what kind of abundance? Financial? Social? Physical or emotional well-being? Envision how you will make that happen.

Be realistic and specific and make note of what steps you must take to realize your goals. If possible, take one symbolic action on your birthday to represent what you're inviting into your life. Plan for it. For example, if you want to be more creative, then gather the supplies you'll need to spend an hour creating a birthday collage for yourself that represents those aspirations you're inviting into your year. Or, if physical wellness is a goal, then take yourself out for a walk or spend that time stretching indoors with your favorite music on. That one act will symbolize your capacity for making change and taking action to achieve what you want.

ASK FOR A GIFT

While material birthday presents are wonderful, the most fulfilling gifts are those from the heart that offer sentiment, or ones that provide meaningful experiences. If it makes sense, ask your loved ones before your birthday if they would give you a thoughtful, heart-centered gift. You could ask your spouse or partner to write you a poem or prose, or take you on a local outdoor adventure where you've never been. You could ask your children to sing you a song they made up for you or present you with a drawing or photo they took themselves, and you could ask your friend to create a card for you infused with good wishes or to bake you a birthday cake with creative decorations.

TAKE THE DAY OFF

Since your birthday is a major holiday, treat it accordingly and take the day off from your regular routine whether it's related to work or other responsibilities. Plan with enough time so you don't get caught in a situation where you are unable to, or feel guilty for being gone that day. Not asking for time off (or conveniently "forgetting") could be another way you subconsciously sabotage your day. Arrange for the day off as early as possible, don't schedule meetings or doctor visits for that day, and support your team's or family's needs in advance of your one-day absence.

Taking the day off means not checking your work email either. One final point: If you are going to take the day off, try not to schedule any big meetings, events, or appointments the day after your birthday or first thing the next morning. This breathing room will let you fully relax and revel in your day.

OR GO TO WORK AND CELEBRATE

Sometimes, it's not possible to take the day off work. There may be certain responsibilities you must attend to on your birthday, or maybe you just started a new job and can't ask for the day off. If that's the case, then so be it.

For those of you who love your job and consider your colleagues your closest friends, then work can often double as the main source of your social life. In those instances—particularly if you tend to have a solitary life outside of work—celebrating your birthday at work could be optimal.

Let your coworkers know in advance that your birthday is approaching and you'd love to do something fun with them like go out to lunch, get ice cream, or have drinks after work. Although you may feel shy asking for a birthday cake, you can always kick-start the tradition by bringing in cake for others on their birthdays. This helps create a culture of celebration that will spread from person to person when it's their turn to be in the center.

You can also bring in your own birthday cake. While it sounds unconventional, do it with a playful spirit of celebration. Bring the candles, call your friends together, and welcome their sincere pleasure in celebrating you. Everyone is esteemed on their birthday, and everybody else knows it.

Even if your colleagues aren't your closest friends, and if your job is stressing you out and taking the day off will stress you further to the point of making you miserable, then go to work. Leave early if you can or take a longer lunch and make sure your coworkers know it's your birthday. That way, the birthday spirit can still be part of your day, even though it's a pressured, work-filled day.

THE BIRTHDAY SPIRIT AT WORK

When Samira turned thirty-two, she had to work on her birthday. She had important meetings scheduled throughout the day and couldn't take the day off without creating negative consequences. Her colleagues knew it was her birthday—she made sure to remind them—and little surprises came her way. A bouquet of wildflowers showed up on her desk, people wished her happy birthday at meetings and in the hallways, and in the afternoon, colleagues gathered with candles and cake in the break room.

That evening, Samira went to dinner with her family at her favorite restaurant, and by the end of her birthday, even though she couldn't take the day off, she felt fully celebrated and uplifted by all the sweet little moments throughout the day.

WITH WHOM DO YOU WANT TO CELEBRATE?

Assuming you've taken the day off and are able to create the day that you want, think about the people you'd like to spend time with on your birthday. Is there anyone noteworthy?

We often have favorite people in our lives that we rarely see. These are souls with whom we closely resonate—who often feel like family to us—yet aren't in the intimate day-to-day orbit of our lives. Consider your birthday an excellent opportunity to connect with those people. Whomever you do choose to see on your birthday, be sure they help you feel the most positive and bring you the most enjoyment.

A HEALING FRIENDSHIP

Maria loved celebrating her birthday and always tried to think of new experiences to enjoy. One year, when her birthday fell midweek, Maria decided to ask Lily, her acupuncturist, to meet her for breakfast before she had to go to the clinic. Lily was a smart woman with a warm personality, a fun sense of humor, and a lot of depth. She and Maria "clicked" the first time they met, and always hit it off during their appointments.

So even though it was unorthodox, Maria ventured outside her comfort zone to ask Lily if she'd join her for a birthday breakfast. Lily was delighted to accept—especially since her birthday was one week earlier—and they had a wonderful, uplifting time together. That experience began an annual tradition where they now meet once a year to celebrate their birthdays together.

CELEBRATE DURING BIRTHDAY WEEK

Since your birthday is so spiritually aligned, it's essential to celebrate yourself on your actual birthday. However, many circumstances can prevent the full celebration you'd like to have. That's when Birthday Week comes in handy. While you are still celebrating your birthday on the real day, you can make other types of birthday plans on the days leading up to and directly after your birthday.

While Birthday Week is the backup for when there's too much to fit into your actual day, or when ideal plans aren't as convenient as they could be, don't let it eclipse doing something special on your actual birthday.

IT'S MY PARTY

Trey was a recent convert to realizing the power of birthdays. When he turned thirty-two and first celebrated his birthday as if it were a major holiday, it changed his entire outlook and birthday experience. It was fun. It was powerful. He was hooked.

The next year when he turned thirty-three, he organized a party at a billiards hall. His birthday fell on a Saturday that year, but he planned the party for Friday night so his colleagues could join him after work. In his mind, that would leave him all day Saturday to celebrate too. He was going to have crawfish flown in from Louisiana and spend his actual birthday enjoying a crawfish boil with his cousin.

Trey had a wonderful time at the billiards party even though he could feel it wasn't aligned with his actual day. Nevertheless, everyone came to celebrate him and had fun. But sure enough, the next day, his birthday fell flat. He was tired and spent from the night before, and a big storm in Louisiana prevented the crawfish from being overnighted in time. What's more, Trey's cousin got sick, and since his friends had already celebrated with him the night before, he didn't want to ask them to celebrate with him again.

Trey ended up having a disappointing day on his actual birthday and then realized that he had made a mistake: He should have held his billiards party on Saturday night with whichever friends could make it. He committed at that moment to always celebrate his birthday on his actual day so that he could fully benefit from the spiritual alignment and power of the day.

CELEBRATE ON A BUDGET

While it is true that many trappings of the typical birthday celebration require money, it does not have to be that way. The most satisfying birthdays can be enjoyed without a lot of money. It's about the richness of the experience.

If you're looking for ways to celebrate your own birthday without spending money, go on a hike with friends, stroll the riverfront, visit the park, browse the farmers' market, wander around your city as if you were a tourist, or have a potluck dinner party and play board games or charades. Just make sure someone's assigned to bring the cake.

A GARDEN PARTY

Anna is a single mother whose birthday is in mid-May. The year she turned twenty-six, her family visited to celebrate. Since they spent a lot of money paying for the flights and rental car, Anna wanted to celebrate without spending too much money—theirs or hers.

She decided to visit a local farm that was holding a flower sale that weekend. It was a beautiful place nestled along a creek, and Anna packed a picnic lunch so they could spend the afternoon at the farm. Her family brought the cake.

They all had a relaxed time together and laughed a lot recounting stories from their past. Her family bought Anna some plants that she planted in her garden later that day, and whenever she tended the plants throughout the year, they reminded her of the simple, lovely, and happy birthday celebration that she shared with her family.

The same approach can hold true when it comes to celebrating your friends. Rather than buying a gift for a friend, make them a collage card and write them a poem about the three qualities you value most about them. If they are a parent, give them "gift certificates" where you offer them childcare or help with gardening, doing laundry, or grocery shopping.

Also, while budgetary concerns may be genuine—and worth respecting—pay attention to how you spend money during the rest of the year. Do you believe you don't have enough money to celebrate yourself, yet find the money to spend on other items and other people throughout the year that are not as essential? If so, then find a way to prioritize your budgeting so that some money can be set aside to celebrate your day in the way you prefer. If the money's there for other uses, then it can be there for you as well. All it takes is good planning.

All told, the old saying is true: The best things in life are free (though they might not always be easy to come by). Just think of the last time you had a really good belly laugh.

THROW A PARTY

If you're going to throw yourself a birthday party (or if one is being thrown for you), think about the guest list. We often mistakenly think that birthday parties are ideal opportunities to bring everyone together from different parts of our life. However, when that happens, we sometimes don't feel the harmonious social chemistry we'd like, and it can feel awkward and weigh down our birthday spirit.

Since we're extra sensitive on our birthdays, be thoughtful about which friends you'd like to bring together and how many people you can handle in one room. Some of us prefer more intimate gatherings and some of us like big "include everyone" parties. As long as you're mindful about what you're creating (versus operating out of habit or obligatory assumptions), then chances are you'll enjoy your own party.

Keep this in mind: When throwing a big party, you'll typically spend less time socializing with your closest friends. That's because the friends you see less often will understandably want face time with you and you'll want, or feel like, you have to share your time with them. If you'd like an intimate social experience on your birthday, don't throw a big party; create a small one.

Depending on how much social time you want to devote to your celebration, one option is to have breakfast or lunch with one or two friends who can provide the meaningful intimacy you'd like to have, and then have a larger party later in the evening, which could take several forms. Perhaps you'd like friends over for drinks; or maybe it's dinner at a favorite restaurant; or even simpler, it can be an after-dinner "cake party" where friends come over for an hour or two at the end of the evening to partake in the birthday cake ritual. All of this depends on a variety of factors and what you'd like to create.

If you prefer to be spontaneous on your birthday, that's fine as long as you're thoughtful about the potential consequences. If you'd like to include people in your plans, inform them with enough advance notice so they can participate. As mentioned earlier, being spontaneous can be one subconscious way we sabotage our birthday since it could mean no one is available to celebrate with us at the last minute.

WELCOME THE BIRTHDAY SPIRIT

Birthdays are actually three days long. The day before, the day of, and the day after. If you're paying attention, you can feel the birthday spirit starting to materialize as the eve of your birthday approaches. Be mindful of what you do on your birthday eve and find ways to welcome the spirit. Tend to your birthday altar. Put on music and dance. Or do something mellow like journaling.

Try to be sensitive to your mood and desires. Say no to mundane tasks that may weigh you down or to interactions with friends or family that may impact your energy in ways that feel depleting. You are beginning to lighten and change your resonance. Let yourself indulge in those rituals and interactions that nourish you, so that when you wake up on your birthday you feel ready for the day in full glory. The birthday spirit will alter you. And that's the point.

The day after your birthday, you will still feel the shimmering presence of the birthday spirit. That day is for integrating what happened the day before and for basking in the good feelings you hopefully experienced. The birthday spirit will continue to hover the day after your birthday before it gently fades away as the evening descends.

GET INTO THE GROOVE

Luna loved celebrating her birthday. Just before turning twenty-five, she took a last-minute ski trip with her family, which coincided with her birthday. Although she was having fun with everyone, she felt flat inside as her birthday eve approached. For some reason, she wasn't feeling excited for her birthday the next day and could not summon the birthday spirit that usually appeared once evening fell. What could she do? She let it go.

Fortunately, everyone went to sleep early that night and she found herself alone. Now was her chance. She lit some candles, assembled her birthday altar with items she brought from home, and played some concert recordings of her favorite band.

Her best friend texted birthday eve greetings and noted she was listening to the same band. So, with a few more texts, they aligned the show to begin playing at the same time and enjoyed the music together while remaining in their own spaces. They danced and texted about various songs. By the end of the first set, as midnight descended, Luna was thoroughly energized and uplifted, ready to welcome in her special day. She thanked her friend for helping her raise the birthday spirit.

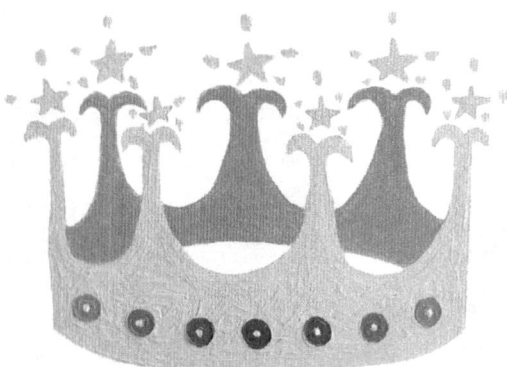

4

CELEBRATE THE DAY

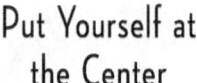

Put Yourself at the Center

Now that you understand the value of preparing for your birthday and are ready to embrace a sacredly abundant day, here are some ideas for ways to celebrate. Although they are grouped under morning, midday, and evening hours, they can be done whenever you like.

MORNING RITUALS

Honor Your Spirit

Find time in the day—ideally first thing in the morning—to connect with your spirit, which is the vibrant, breathing, peaceful essence that inhabits your form, way beyond the learned personality, beliefs, and behaviors that society imposes on us.

Sit in silence for just a few minutes to connect to that soothing place inside. This practice provides a valuable opportunity that will help you get centered enough to receive the external energies that will come your way as the day unfolds. Even if it's literally just for one minute, acknowledging this mighty, humble presence that inhabits the person called "you" will put you into spiritual alignment and prepare you for a harmonious day.

Other ways to honor your spirit:

• Phone home. Prayer is the most direct way to connect to our Higher Self. By engaging in prayerful thought, we satisfy the deep longing of our spirit to reunite with our spiritual source from which we separated at birth.

• Light a candle or stick of incense on your birthday altar and spend some meditative moments staring at the flame or curling smoke.

• Go for a walk in nature and open your senses to be as fully present as possible.

• Sit in the garden or on your fire escape with your morning tea or coffee and be receptive to the energy around you.

• Visit your preferred place of worship or spiritually powerful place.

• Read from a spiritually uplifting book.

• Pull an angel card or tarot card that offers you a word or theme to represent the year ahead. You can focus on a question or just affirm that the message the cards will reveal is one that supports your highest self during the year ahead. [*The Original Angel Cards* by Kathy Tyler are simple and lovely and available online.]

• Ask yourself: For what am I grateful for in this life? What is the one thing I wish I could change in my life that I have the power to change?

Once we connect with our Higher Self, even briefly, we have fed and honored our spirit so that our human self can savor the rest of the day and not feel like we're missing something on our birthday. Indeed, making that sacred connection brings an immediate feeling of grace that will flow throughout the rest of the day.

Honor Your Body

As noted earlier, our body is our spirit's true marriage partner. From the day we're born, it's Spirit + Body 'til death do we part. Our birthday is the anniversary of that marriage, and our birthday should always contain some element that acknowledges and honors the body by doing something that feels physically good.

Suggestions include these:

• Take a warm bath with fragrant essential oils and emotionally stirring music.

• Stretch. Taking just ten minutes to slow down and focus on your breathing, while gently stretching, effectively enlivens and awakens the body. Don't stretch till it hurts, just stretch until you hit that point that feels good. It requires tuning in, but that's the whole point—it's time to tune into the body and honor its role in your life.

• Engage in your favorite activity. Soccer? Tennis? Yoga? Canoe? Pickleball? Bike ride? If you love it and it feels good, go do it on your birthday.

- Dance. Whether dancing around your living room in the morning or going out with friends to a dance club at night, few activities generate as much joy as dancing to your favorite music. If dancing is something you love to do, then find a way to dance on your birthday.

- Eat your favorite foods whether you prepare them yourself or buy them elsewhere. Fully savor the flavors and experience. Treat yourself to what you love.

- Adorn yourself. Since you are officially birthday royalty, put on a fabulous outfit and make yourself look as spectacular as you want to feel. Wear your favorite scent or essential oil; put on your favorite piece of jewelry. Wear your favorite hat. Dress up like the divine being you are.

Honor Your Parents

Our parents are the reason we are here. So when it's your birthday, take the time to acknowledge them (whether in person or in spirit) and thank them for ushering you into this world. One way to honor your parents is to send them flowers—especially your mother. The mother/child bond is the strongest human bond there is, and on your birthday, there is much connection and love to be felt by honoring your mother and thanking her for bringing you into this life.

If you have a strained relationship with your parents, find a way to acknowledge them anyway, if only in your mind and heart. Doing so can bring a glimmer of healing, and that opening, however small, can bring you forward in your personal story. If, however, there is too much pain in your family history to do this, then use the power of your birthday to help you let go of this upsetting relationship so that you can continue forward with your life, with as much healing goodness as you can create for yourself.

MIDDAY RITUALS

Tell Strangers It's Your Birthday

While your friends and colleagues may already know it's your birthday—whether you've told them directly or indirectly via social media—also tell the strangers you come across in your day. Mention it to the associate at the bakery or the neighbor walking their dog. Do it with sincere enthusiasm and a sense of mirth and watch what happens.

Everyone lights up when it's somebody's birthday. By telling strangers it's your birthday, you'll receive their positive energy that they are naturally happy to give you. Plus, you're including them in something meaningful, and their bright smile is the spiritual gift they can give you. Play with it and see what happens. It's a rare soul that won't light up and wish you a sincere "Happy Birthday."

By telling others it's your birthday, it helps make your birthday more real so that you're actually on board for it. It's interesting how often our birthdays can come and go without our really feeling like it's our special day. It takes intention and effort to bring our birthdays to life so that they fulfill us.

Be Creative

Carve out some time for creative expression. Creative energy is our birthright, and everyone is able to participate in it. If you create something tangible, let it be something that commemorates your birthday and place it on your birthday altar.

Buy Yourself a Gift

While truly fulfilling birthdays are spiritual in nature, there's always room for gifts. The world is full of natural gifts (the stunning display of pink-hued clouds, the uplifting fragrance of honeysuckle) and our birthdays can be made more pleasurable with material gifts as well. However, the gifts should be the spice, not the main ingredient.

When buying yourself a birthday gift, think about the ideal item that will memorialize your day and bring happiness throughout the year. Focus on something you would have fun shopping for and spend some time finding your birthday present even if you don't know what it will be until you see it. But if you hate shopping, then don't do it. Instead, buy some flowers or a houseplant as a loving gesture you make for yourself.

You buy gifts for others; allow yourself to buy a gift for yourself. You can always buy your gift during Birthday Week or some other time close to your actual day. Just be clear about the intention and let the gift remind you of your birthday.

If money is hard to come by, then save for your gift. It doesn't need to cost a lot, and many inexpensive items can still be pleasing. Don't buy something "just because," but if you find something alluring, then buy it with a full heart. And if someone gives you birthday money, set some aside to buy yourself a gift even though it may be tempting to use it to pay the bills. Again, a gift doesn't have to cost much, and it shows you value yourself while bringing a feeling of importance to the day that is just for you.

If you enjoy shopping (or love shopping a bit too much), try not to let the shopping experience dominate. Give it no more than an hour or two or else it will crowd out other experiences that can bring a richer meaning to your day. By making time for the magical moments of a birthday, you will feel an expanded sense of happiness and fulfillment as the day unfolds and passes. Besides, you can always shop any other day of the year.

One final note about shopping: If you are a sensitive soul, you are likely impacted by the vibes of the environment around you. Since birthdays open us up to feeling extra sensitive, choose to shop at places that lift your spirit. Neighborhood shopping streets or local boutiques tend to have a nurturing spirit. Pay attention to this and see how these venues make you feel. Shop gently.

If you really don't want to spend money on yourself, then consider making a donation to your favorite charity. "Doing good feels good," and this is a noble way to celebrate your presence on the planet. Be careful, though, not to make a donation as a way to avoid receiving on your birthday. If you actually do want a gift for yourself but feel guilty about it, then that's all the more reason you should buy the gift. Put yourself first on your birthday. It's the one day a year you're given 100 percent permission to do that.

EVENING RITUALS

Have Cake

For most of us, the birthday cake tradition started in childhood. It's an engaging ritual that allows for a focused moment of celebration. Bringing out the birthday cake, lit with candles while singing "Happy Birthday to You" is typically the height of our traditional birthday festivities and holds tremendous value. Even if you think it doesn't matter, having a birthday cake does matter and glorifies the birthday spirit.

If you're celebrating your birthday with friends, partners, roommates, neighbors, or colleagues, let them bring you birthday cake and sing to you. Usually, people know to do this on your behalf, so if they offer, welcome the gesture openly. Don't sabotage your birthday by telling people you don't want cake. No matter how old you are, it's always a moment filled with love.

If you're concerned no one will take the initiative to bring you a cake, there are several solutions. First, you can ask for what you want. Even though it can feel like a vulnerable request, people are often delighted to support our happy birthdays and feel honored that they get to provide the cake.

The second option is to provide your own cake. It's perfectly fine to invite people over to celebrate your birthday and have your own cake on hand, and the happy occasion presents an opportunity to buy a cake from your favorite bakery. If you're in the mood, you can spend part of the day baking and decorating your cake, infusing it with all your good energy and intentions. Either way, find a way to have a cake with candles.

Blowing out your candles, just after you make your wish, is another ritual that holds meaning. By now, you should have been thinking about your birthday wish and the kind of energy or experience you'd like to bring into your new year. Affirming that wish just before you blow out the candles is a powerful act of magic infused with your clear and focused intentions. Let yourself have that moment, each and every year.

Some years, our birthdays may be more solitary in nature. For reasons that vary, we may find ourselves alone on our birthdays. If this is one of those years, bake or buy yourself a cake or a cupcake and put candles on it. Sing to yourself or stream "Happy Birthday to You" online, make your wish, and blow out your candles. While doing this ritual alone may sound heartbreaking, a broken heart is an open heart. You'll be in a position to feel a lot of self-love and compassion, which, in itself, is the most powerful and poignant birthday gift of all.

If you're celebrating your birthday at a restaurant, let the server know it's your birthday, if your friends haven't already done so. They'll often bring out candles on a cake at the end of the meal. Some restaurants make a big production of birthdays with several staff coming out to sing to you. If you know of a restaurant like this, go there to celebrate and receive the love. Even if it's from strangers, the moment is pure and genuine.

Some people are uncomfortable during the birthday song and want to silence it before it even happens. While you might feel self-conscious to be the center of attention while people sing to you in public, let it happen. It's a moment of honor, and everyone around is uplifted by it as well. If you feel emotion welling up, let it out. Why not?

If your birthday is close to someone else's birthday such as a roommate or friend, and you're given the option, let yourself have your own birthday cake, and let them have theirs. While it's tempting to share the spotlight out of concern that it's too much for others to do for you, let yourself have your day anyway. Group birthday celebrations are fine if that's what's being offered, but if given the choice, everyone deserves their own solo in the middle of the dance floor.

Make a Birthday Wish

The birthday wish is one of the most important elements of a full, satisfying birthday. It's our gift from the Universe. The birthday wish allows us to think about the qualities, experiences, or achievements we'd like in the coming year and throw it up to the heavens as our own personal prayer. Indeed, meditating on the birthday wish is a valuable ritual that provides us with an opportunity for spiritual centering. Spend moments in the morning or throughout the day thinking about what you'd like to manifest in the coming year. Let that be the basis of your birthday wish.

When we ponder our birthday wish, it tells us what we genuinely desire in life, at that time in our life. Is it partnership?

Love? Happier relationships? Money and abundance? Health? Creative expression? Friends? Fulfillment at work? Courage to make the necessary changes in our life? Whatever it is, it's a window into our soul's desire. With each year passing, isn't it time to do what we can to fulfill this yearning in our life? The birthday wish gives us an opportunity to focus on that yearning.

Keep your birthday wish personal in nature and make sure it's concrete and attainable. Altruism is a good thing, but often it's a noble way we conveniently avoid receiving. So, while it's admirable to wish for world peace, try to avoid doing that on your birthday and allow yourself to focus on what you wish to have in a more personal way. Perhaps it's for more peace in your relationships or with your inner self. Or perhaps it's for more serenity and meditative moments that help you feel more peaceful in the world.

Try to keep your birthday wish general enough while still being specific. This helps cast a wide net onto the future that allows the Universe to more readily manifest our desire. If we're too specific about what we want, it can cloud our recognition of an answered wish because that answer doesn't look exactly like what we wished for. Often what we think we want isn't what ultimately serves us the most.

Consider this: Rather than wishing to fall in love with someone who hasn't shown up in your life yet, wish for an abundant, joyous social life full of loving people you already know—and have yet to meet—while trusting you will always remain open for that special someone whenever they appear.

What's most essential is that the wish is attainable through our own actions. For example, when wishing for a more abundant social life, we can take many actions in the coming year to fulfill that wish, rather than waiting passively for new friends to show up in our life. Indeed, by making wishes that we can achieve ourselves, we take our power and responsibility and focus our intention to create the potential for fulfillment.

While it is wise to keep our wishes focused, yet general in nature, it is possible to make a specific wish as long as it seems attainable and serves as an inspiration toward that goal. Let's say you're working on a book—or any other creative endeavor that requires more of your attention and devotion to complete—then using your birthday to wish for completion of that effort is a good wish. It encapsulates both a desire for more creative effort and acknowledges the power you have in making your wish come true. The fact that you used your birthday wish to call forth that completion means you have extra magic and commitment backing up your will to succeed.

Make the wish affirmative. Whenever we want something in life, it's wise to state it affirmatively. Whether a New Year's resolution, a birthday wish, or even just a reminder note to yourself, state it in the positive. For example, rather than posting a note in your kitchen that says "Don't forget to feed the fish," say, instead, "Remember to feed the fish." Affirm the action you want (remembering) versus the action you're trying to move away from (forgetting).

Keep your wish to yourself. Our birthday wish is personal and reflects our innermost desires. While you might be tempted to share your wish, try to refrain. This is because there is power in keeping thoughts private. It's an energy that remains contained within you and doesn't "leak" in the sharing of it. Another reason to keep your birthday wish private is that if you know you will keep it to yourself, you can be more truthful with your wish, rather than making sure it's "palatable and noble" to others. Holding your wish close lets you really be honest with what you desire.

When it comes time to make your actual birthday wish, do so with your birthday cake and candles. If you prefer to make your birthday wish at another time, be mindful of the ritual surrounding it. One powerful time to focus on your wish is during the minute that you were born. If you know your time of birth, it may work well for you to use that exact time each year to focus on your intentions and birthday wish for the coming year. Most birth certificates have the time of birth written on them. You can request a copy by contacting your birth state's vital records office.

5

WHAT NOT TO DO ON YOUR BIRTHDAY

Support Your Chances for a Happy Day

Now that you know the healing power of creating ritual and celebration for your birthday, here are a few bits of wisdom to keep in mind so that your best laid plans don't go awry.

AVOID DRAINING CONVERSATIONS

Try to steer clear of distressing conversations the night before your birthday and on your birthday. As your sensitivity will be heightened, your skin will be thin and you'll feel your energy drop if you engage in conversations that are stressful or negative for whatever reason.

The kinds of conversations that can wait until after your birthday deal with finances, relationship challenges, health issues, job stress, gossip, and complaints. Instead, focus your intention on positive conversations. If you're called to explore the meaning of life on your birthday, and it has some profound implications, that's different. That's beautiful. That type of exploration promises redemption if you stick with it long enough, no matter how deep it gets.

When I turned fifty-one, I had a heavy birthday. Two weeks earlier, my twenty-three-year-old cousin had died by suicide, and my family was plunged into profound sorrow. The reverberations of his death were felt deeply, and we were all left grappling with many unanswered questions. I kept wishing we could press the rewind button and go back for a do-over.

Then, three days before my birthday, I received more devastating news. Another cousin—one of my best friends and most treasured people in the world—told me he had a large tumor on his pancreas that spread to his liver. He was sixty-seven and knew it was not likely he would survive much longer. His biopsy was performed on my birthday, and the doctor confirmed it was stage 4 pancreatic cancer and that the prognosis was not good.

My morning was spent receiving birthday calls from my family that quickly turned into conversations about cousin David's cancer and the shock and sadness we felt. Throughout the day, although I was able to engage in my ritualized birthday celebrations like listening to music, having lunch at my favorite café, buying myself a pretty gift, writing this actual vignette, and having a lovely dinner with my husband and two friends, I felt a heaviness in my soul. I wasn't in the mood to be lighthearted or "up." I was feeling grief at the thought of losing my beloved cousin (especially so soon after the tragic death of my other dear cousin), and this birthday, this age, was going to memorialize that moment for me for the rest of my life.

So what did I do? I cried. I wrote. I used the power of my birthday to ask myself yet again: "Tamar, what do you really want to do for the rest of your life?" I used that moment of deep sadness within me and my family to recommit to the life I wanted to live for myself. The presence of death was a wake-up call for me. Life is precious. Life is fleeting. Life is ours to create to the best of our ability.

DON'T BE ATTACHED TO PERFECTION

While it's exciting to plan for our birthdays, sometimes our plans don't manifest the way we intended. It's surprising to realize how much we script our lives. We imagine exactly what our friends will say to us and how witty we will be when it's our turn to speak. We envision how we'll feel and act at some future point, and we never realize how attached we are to the script we're playing in our mind. This is particularly true on our birthdays.

We've planned everything we can, yet, when the day shows up, it's always different than we imagined it. The setting might be perfect, but our energy might feel off. Or a friend might disappoint us. Or the weather might interfere. Or on the other hand, fabulous occurrences might happen that we didn't expect and we don't know how to integrate them because we didn't script them.

Surprisingly, wonderful experiences can throw us off our center too. Do your best to prepare for what you want, and, then, when the day arrives, let go of perfection, let go of the control, and let your birthday flow in ways that will surprise and delight you. Just try to stay in the moment and enjoy.

HAVE YOUR CAKE AND EAT IT TOO

Marcia was looking forward to celebrating her birthday with a special birthday cake she'd been eyeing in the bakery window for months. As her birthday approached, she homed in on just the right flavor combination and icing color. She placed her order two weeks in advance, and after a birthday-morning manicure, she excitedly went to the bakery to pick up her special cake. Unfortunately, they got her order wrong.

She was understandably upset. How could they get her order wrong when she was so intentional and clear about it? Even worse, she didn't receive any sympathy from the harried baker behind the counter. She wanted to file a complaint with the owner of the bakery and write a scathing online review for this hugely disappointing mishap. She was so distraught by this unexpected setback—especially since she had planned for her perfect cake for so long—that it took all the joy out of her birthday.

As the soured hours passed, she realized she had a choice to make: she could accept her disappointment and let it go, or let it ruin her entire day. She chose to let it go. She ended up salvaging her birthday by focusing on the situations in her life she was most grateful for and realized that, while we can't control what happens to us, we can control our attitude about it. She learned a lot about herself that day, which was an unexpected and valuable birthday gift.

DON'T TURN THE RITUAL INTO A RUT

Rituals are powerful ways to acknowledge big moments and raise spiritual energy. However, look at most religions and you'll see where divinely inspired rituals have become so routine that they fail to accomplish what they were intended to do. Don't let your birthday ritual become a rut. How will you know if that's happened? You'll find yourself dogmatically attached to the ritual and you'll miss the expansive vibrancy you used to feel.

While some birthday ceremonies (like cake and birthday wishes) are very important to enact every year, even these rituals can turn rote when you start feeling like you have to do it a certain way year after year. Craft your birthday, but beware the trap of birthday routine. Let your birthday rituals feel fresh and uplifting.

DON'T LET YOUR PARTNER BRING YOU DOWN

Relationships can be complicated. Despite falling in love with someone and committing to forever, relationships can be fraught with unmet needs. These unmet needs are often sub-conscious in nature and, whether they are recognized or not, eventually create hurt feelings. Over time, when these hurt feelings remain unattended to, they harden into resentment, which is like scar tissue on the heart. Not fun.

Since birthdays are our own personal major holiday—the one day the world officially gets to revolve around us—it is a perfect, if unfortunate, moment for our partners to act out the resentments they feel for us and not participate in our joy. As such, they exhibit forgetfulness, apathy, or, worse, active rejection of whatever it is we ask of them, however simple it is.

HELLO, FOLLY!

Lottie was celebrating her sixty-sixth birthday at home. She and her husband, Barnes, were travel-ing for the holidays the day after her birthday and decided that a low-key birthday, with just the two of them, was a good choice before they hit the road. Lottie thought about what would make her happy and let Barnes know her wishes.

Lottie was a big fan of old Hollywood musicals, so after a nice birthday dinner with a good bottle of wine and a festive birthday cake, she went to watch a musical in the den—something she'd been looking forward to for days. Barnes didn't join her. He hated musicals and couldn't stomach another round of *Meet Me in St. Louis*. So Lottie went off on her own, much to her deep disappointment. It was her birthday after all. Couldn't her husband support her simple birthday wishes and show up for her—especially when she asked?

About twenty minutes after the movie started, Lottie's sister-in-law called to wish her a happy birthday. Barnes picked up the phone, and when his sister learned that Lottie was watching her birthday movie alone, she peppered Barnes with questions: Why wasn't he watching the movie with her? Why wasn't he sitting next to her, holding her hand while she sang along to "Have Yourself a Merry Little Christmas?" Why was he denying his wife such a simple pleasure on her birthday?

Barnes and his sister were close, and after some back and forth, he finally admitted that he'd been harboring some resentment toward his wife. As a successful literary agent, Lottie often worked late nights and focused on her work with a passion Barnes often wished was directed toward him instead. He felt as if he wasn't getting his own needs met in the relationship, and as he further reflected inwardly, he realized that this resentment made it hard for him to show up for his wife on her birthday. Instead, he was acting out. By not participating in the spirit of celebration that Lottie craved, he was subconsciously "getting her back" and causing her pain. He was sabotaging her birthday joy. Sadly, it worked.

Fortunately, it wasn't too late. Barnes's sister told him to get off the phone and go join his wife on the couch for the rest of the movie. She encouraged him to have a heart-to-heart conversation with Lottie about his feelings—but on another day. Today was her day, and he had the power to lift her spirits by being by her side with love and support. So that's what he did. And Lottie ended up having a happy birthday after all.

Consider your birthday an annual thermometer that helps you gauge the temperature of your relationship. If your partner refuses to celebrate your day the way you would like, it's time to do some deep soul-searching. Where in your relationship is negativity allowed to exist? Does it show up as outward hostility and anger or does it cloak itself in funny sarcasm, teasing put-downs, and just-kidding barbs?

Try a new approach with your partner and agree to make your words and interactions as positive as possible. Try to cultivate more appreciation and affection for one another. It's amazing how powerful those attitudes are. They work like magic when offered sincerely—whether in big ways or small.

Having said that, while it's possible there are no hidden agendas in someone's decision to not fully celebrate their partner's birthday, it's hard to understand why someone wouldn't cherish the opportunity to celebrate their beloved one day a year.

DON'T GIVE UP

If your birthday starts off crappy (for reasons under or out of your control), don't give up. The day's not over yet. Allow the negativity to pass through and move on. Then try to reclaim your day and let the goodness bubble up. Turn on the radio and let it serenade you. Amazingly, the radio will sing just the right songs to you on your birthday. Go for a walk in your neighborhood and smile at people.

Look for the positive flow of energy and let it happen. It's there. And if your birthday still ends up being awful for whatever reason you cannot control, feel the pain and let it be okay. Have compassion for yourself.

6

YOUR BIRTHDAY
AND THE HOLIDAYS

Keep Yourself at
the Center

Every once in a while, you or someone in your life is born on a major holiday or close to it. Though in actuality, this alignment makes our birthday extra significant, sharing our birthday with a holiday can pose many challenges that result in us feeling less special on our day.

What should you do if your birthday falls on a holiday? Celebrate anyway. A big holiday should never outdo your own personal major holiday, and you shouldn't put it on hold until the holiday passes. Having said that, if you want to throw a birthday party for yourself, you might want to do that a week before or after to accommodate your friends who may otherwise not be available. Let the holiday provide a birthday theme if you are so inspired.

Whatever holiday celebrations happen, don't let them replace personal celebration on your actual birthday. While it's true that others will be focused on the holiday, allow yourself to ask for what you want and find creative ways to meet those desires.

If your birthday falls on or near a holiday—whether it's a traditional US holiday or one connected to your culture or religion—think about what the holiday symbolizes for you and let it inform the meaning of your life—not just your birthday.

HERE ARE SOME POSSIBLE THEMES TO CONSIDER WHEN BEING BORN CLOSE TO A HOLIDAY

New Year's Day

If you were born on or close to the new year, consider your personal theme one of renewal. If you were born just before January 1, it's possible your life's theme has more to do with resolution and completion than if you were born after January 1, which might be more about creating and initiating. Either way, honoring endings and beginnings as a natural part of change and renewal could be a way to navigate your own personal new year.

Valentine's Day

If your birthday falls near this heart-filled day, then consider your personal theme to be love. Who are the people and what are the experiences and causes that you love? By putting your heart into your life (such as your work, your pursuits, your family, your friends, your acquisitions), you will be rewarded with wonderful satisfaction that comes from being centered in love.

April Fool's Day

If you were born on April Fool's Day, consider your personal theme to be lighthearted. Where in your life can you allow for more silliness and laughter? While it's true that life is not a joke, sometimes it is! Work with the symbolism of this day to experience some expansive uplift in those more serious sides of your life.

Easter

If your birthday aligns with Easter, then consider your personal theme one of rebirth. Much like springtime when life regenerates anew, allow yourself to consider all the ways you can rise up from outdated versions of yourself that are ready to be released so new growth can occur.

Memorial Day

If your birthday falls near Memorial Day, consider your personal theme to be one of remembering. Whether it is your ancestors, a moment of global history that touches you, or your personal history, bringing honor and respect to those memories will help you integrate what they represent to you. Remembering the past is a powerful way to help direct the future.

Juneteenth and Independence Day

If your birthday falls near Juneteenth or the Fourth of July, consider your personal theme to be one of freedom. What

condition or situation in your life requires the most freedom
for you to live up to your full potential? Where do you need
more independence to flourish? Declare your autonomy and
write your own rules. Your life belongs to you.

Labor Day

If your birthday falls near Labor Day, consider your personal
theme to be industriousness. You have a lot of energy in this
life to work hard and get stuff done. Focus on those events
that bring you the most pleasure, and the fruits of your labor
will be sweet.

Halloween

If you were born on or near Halloween, consider your personal theme to be magic. How do you experience your inner
power and charm? What can you do to enhance the magical qualities in your life in order to manifest what you truly
desire? Let your birthday wish be the spell you cast for the
coming year.

Thanksgiving

If you were born around Thanksgiving (every year it will be
different), then consider your personal theme to be gratitude.
Being thankful for all the goodness in your life (even if there
is difficulty involved) is a proven recipe for physical, mental,
and emotional wellness. Adopting an attitude of gratitude is
truly transformational.

Winter Solstice, Hanukkah, Christmas, and Kwanzaa

If your birthday falls around these wintertime holidays that occur near the darkest time of the year in the Northern Hemisphere, then consider your personal theme to be light. What lights you up in life? How do you best share your own radiance with others? Kindling your inner light brings warmth, not just to you, but to the world.

7

CELEBRATE OTHERS

Add Sparkle to the Birthday Spirit

We can find immense joy in celebrating others' birthdays. The trick is realizing that by fully celebrating your own birthday, you become infused with an abundance of satisfaction and sparkle to share with others when it's their turn. Spirit builds spirit, so celebrating others is a powerful act of love and affirmation that reverberates back to you on your own birthday in a positive feedback loop.

CELEBRATE YOUR SPOUSE OR PARTNER

Celebrating your partner's birthday should be an honored opportunity to treasure them. There are many ways to do this, and, again, like any holiday, the event requires planning:

• Decorate the house. Put up a "Happy Birthday" banner to surprise them in the morning and display childhood photos on their birthday altar.

• Indulge them throughout the day with a pep talk like, "YOU are the Birthday King/Queen." Whatever they want that day, they get. Be happily in service to them.

• Let them know how important the day is for you too. Share your gratitude for their presence in your life.

• Be upbeat and expansive for them. Since birthdays can evoke feelings of melancholy, lead the way by celebrating your partner's day with joy. Your energy will set a positive tone.

• Plan ahead. Just as you should do with yourself, plan their birthday a month before—unless it's a big birthday that requires a lot more planning. Ask what they'd like to do. They don't have to know at that time, but by getting the conversation started, the ideas can begin to flow and the planning can begin.

• Honor their request. If your partner says they hate surprise parties, then don't throw one. Alternately, you may know that secretly they'd love a surprise party. If that's the case, start plotting.

• If they're feeling melancholy as their day approaches, talk about it. Explore their fears around aging, disappointments, feeling spiritually unfulfilled or unworthy. You don't need to have the answers, but by opening the dialogue, they might perceive what is blocking them from stepping into the full celebration of their birthday.

• Get them a cake. Whether you bake it or buy it, and even if it's just the two of you, this ritual matters.

• If they have to (or choose to) work that day, help make their normal workday celebratory. Show up and surprise them if you can. Also make sure their close colleagues know it's their birthday so they can offer warm greetings of the day.

• Another sweet ritual is to sit with them early in the morning before they leave for work and give them a thoughtful card or gift. Sharing that moment helps create a loving bond that continues throughout the day.

CELEBRATE FRIENDS

Whether inviting a friend out to dinner, sending a card, or texting a photo of your super cute dog conveying birthday greetings, take the time to honor your friends on their birthdays. What is most important is the gesture. Since we are extra sensitive on our birthdays, simple and sincere efforts from our friends can move us deeply. Think of the kind of attention you welcome from others on your birthday, and offer that kind of attention to your friends on their day.

One simple and endearing gesture is to call and sing "Happy Birthday to You" when they—or their voice mail— answers the phone. It's surprising how touching that can be. If others are around, ask them to join in the singing, whether they know the person or not. The joy is infectious and uplifts the spirit.

Sometimes, when a good friend is having a birthday, we assume we're automatically included in the celebration. Why wouldn't we be? We naturally want to celebrate their presence in our lives and are 100 percent on board to show up with good cheer and party hats. Sometimes our friends want to celebrate their birthdays with us, and sometimes they want to celebrate differently.

Depending on the nature of your friendship, you might already know what your friend would hope or expect, even though you still shouldn't assume they'll celebrate the day with you. If you are not invited, don't make your friend feel guilty. Just celebrate as is.

You can let your friend know that you're aware their birthday is coming up. Ask them what they think they'd like to do. By asking this question far enough in advance, it gives them the time and space to either voice their desire to share some part of the day (or Birthday Week) with you, or to let you know they have other plans happening, even if they're vague and unformed. If they want to include you, they'll let you know. Either way, remain gracious. However, if it's a good friend whom you sense is falling into the birthday blues and says they're not doing much, take that as a sign to get involved. Go have fun.

CELEBRATE COLLEAGUES

Depending on the kind of work environment you have, celebrating birthdays can be a fun workplace ritual. If you manage, or are part of a small team, honoring your colleagues' birthdays is a terrific way to single them out for your appreciation, while being an equal opportunity for everyone on your team. Just commit to being consistent. If you can't celebrate everyone's birthday equally, then don't celebrate them at all. (Though we pretend not to notice or care if we're overlooked on our birthday, we do notice and we care.)

Bring in cake or cupcakes (make it gluten-free if needed) and some freshly cut fruit or whatever else you know people will enjoy eating, get a card signed by the group, and take a few moments to talk about their birthday plans and most favorite birthdays from the past. If you have a really large staff, then celebrate birthdays on the first of the month or during monthly staff meetings. Acknowledge everyone who has a birthday that month and wish them well. While it might not be realistic to bring in cake for so many people, you can still sprinkle good energy in their direction.

CELEBRATE YOUNG CHILDREN

The way a child is treated on their birthday will set the tone for future expectations, disappointments, or fulfillment in years to come. Your guidance in creating meaningful birthday rituals will give them a framework to draw from for the rest of their lives—just as you celebrate other important holidays. Creating a spirit of meaning on their birthday is easy to achieve. It just takes some insight about your child and creative effort.

Children are naturally sensitive, so before all the fun starts, it can be worthwhile to find time in the morning to sit in front of a birthday altar or go into a natural outdoor setting. Tell them this is the day they were born to join your family, and it is always going to be a special day for them and for you. Ask them to think of three things in their life for which they feel grateful. Let that inspire a conversation that deepens the moment for them.

Gratitude is a powerful pathway, and when we can be grateful for the good in our lives, we then find ourselves centered in the moment, cloaked with a sense of well-being. In turn, this comfort feeds the sensitive child and provides them with a spiritual grounding, which is a wonderful way to anchor and ritualize the beginning of a birthday. This approach will prepare your child for a life of more meaningful birthdays that aren't just focused on presents and cake and school parties in the classroom.

CELEBRATE FAMILY

Family relationships by design are complex. At once, our family represents the people we are closest to, yet at the same time families can be composed of people with whom we don't feel any kind of connection, whether it be spiritual, intellectual, emotional, or otherwise.

Family relationships can be full of harmony or full of dysfunction or somewhere in between. Either way, celebrating your family members' birthdays are opportunities to respectfully acknowledge these relationships. Depending upon the connection with each member of your family, you may celebrate them differently or with similar themes.

If your birthday falls on the same day as an immediate family member's birthday (whether you are twins or not), consider the day extra blessed (unless of course you have a negative relationship). Carve out time to celebrate together (if that's possible) in ways that mutually support your shared interests. But also be sure to spend some time apart, so that you can immerse yourself in your own energy and life's purpose.

8

CELEBRATE WITH SERIOUS ILLNESS

A Poignant Time to Share Love

If we are born, we will die. As depressing as that may sound, it can be spiritually soothing to consider that our death is a gateway, not an end. It's all how you look at it. Allowing for the possibility that consciousness continues beyond the vitality of our earthly form is a comforting and energizing thought as we journey through life.

While it's true that we all will pass, some of us are acutely aware of impending death because of a grave illness or being so old that we know our time is coming. When we are ill, or someone close to us is very ill, there is beautiful potential for heart-centered opening. Letting ourselves feel the sadness of imminent loss can open our heart in ways that are deeply healing for all involved.

Many seriously ill people who have almost reached the end of their journey say that during their last months they experience more richness due to the love they gave and the love they received from others. While the grief of saying goodbye to loved ones is wrenching, it means we care deeply. It means we love.

If someone dear to us is having a birthday—even though their life is likely coming to a close—it is all the more poignant to celebrate and raise the spirit. Laugh. Dance. Go to the beach. The mountains. And by all means, acknowledge the power of their birthday and thank them for being born. If they want to talk about their mortality, offer them your compassionate presence. If they want to talk about the cruise they intend on taking next summer, then offer them your packing suggestions. If they are adamant that they don't want to celebrate their birthday, then respect that wish. They are in a completely different phase of life—one few of us can understand until we are there ourselves. Just send them your love, and trust it is enough.

If you would like to present a gift for a person's "final birthday," one meaningful option is to use the significance of the day to write a letter to them expressing all the gratitude you feel for the ways that they have impacted your life. List the qualities they embody that you admire and strive to emulate. Remind them of your favorite times together. Sprinkle in some humor if it comes naturally. And assure them that no matter how life unfolds, you will always think of them with love. Present the letter to them in person if you can, and sit with them while they read it, or read it aloud to them. Even if they have slipped into a deeper form of consciousness and no longer appear to "be there" in the way you always knew them to be, read it anyway. They will still hear you and receive the love.

Once someone has passed, use their birthday as a portal to connect with their spirit. It's a powerful focal point, and with ritual and heart-centered openness, there can be an energetic connection between the two worlds. Buy flowers. Put out photos. Play their favorite music. You know what to do.

In the end, regardless of how many birthdays we do or do not have ahead of us, it's all about sweet love. If you knew that your life would end soon, how would that change your outlook, your choices, and your love for others and yourself? Let each birthday you celebrate be a moment to ask that question. And make a commitment to yourself to live your life like you want to and to open your heart just a little bit more. Because, behind the curtain, the truth is that love is all there is. And love will always see you through.

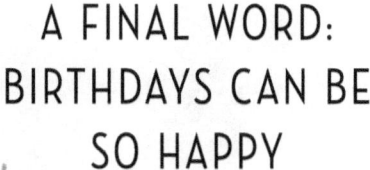

A FINAL WORD:
BIRTHDAYS CAN BE
SO HAPPY

Now that you understand the deeper reasons for celebrating your birthday, I hope you begin to notice the spark that emerges once a year before your birthday arrives. I hope you welcome the spiritual potential of your birthday, allow yourself to enjoy planning how you want to celebrate, and embrace the entire ritual as you make it real.

Take ownership of your birthday to ensure you have the best possible day. Let yourself be happy and you'll see how happy your birthday can be!

HOW TO PLAN YOUR HAPPY BIRTHDAY

A Workbook for Insight, Inspiration, and Ideas

Create the proper time and space to answer the questions posed in this workbook section, chapter by chapter. It is important to write your responses, not just answer them in your mind. If this is your copy of the book, you may use the blank pages (please don't write in the book if you have the library's copy; use a separate sheet of paper).

Write quickly, without editing. Consider this to be a crucial conversation you will have with yourself to bring insight. Be fearless in your exploration and let what emerges inspire you to heal those parts of you that are ready for transformation.

DIG DEEPLY
Expose What's Hidden

Let's first explore the fears, disappointments, and negative ideas most of us likely have around aging and our birthdays. By bringing them into our awareness, we can begin to transform those beliefs into something more positive.

1. Why am I uncomfortable with my birthday?

2. What am I afraid of losing as I age?

Address the physical, mental, emotional, and social spheres of your life.

3. Where am I attached to an idealized vision of my past self? What age is that version of me? What did I have then that I think I don't have now? Why is that quality still so valuable to me?

4. What part of me might believe I don't really deserve to be fully loved and celebrated? Where does that belief come from? Who really owns it?

We often inherit beliefs from our family, friends, religion, media, or community without realizing it, so it's powerful to "return" those beliefs to the source that generated it. When we realize that so much of what we carry around isn't really ours, we are given permission to let go of those inhibiting, self-denying beliefs.

5. Why do I think my birthdays are or can be such a challenge?

Ideally, the answers you've just written will give you insights that help you answer this question. Once you realize why your birthdays can be so challenging, you are prepared to actually create and have a happy birthday.

6. Where are the areas of my life where I may be squan-
   dering this nonrenewable resource called time or life?

This last question is a general one that helps bring awareness
to your life overall. It's useful when thinking about your birthday, and beyond. Make a list of all the ways you waste time in
your life. It could be in the emotional or mental sphere (like
worrying too much about what you can't control), or it could
be time spent interacting with technology (like spending too
much time on social media or watching reality TV). Whatever
it is, write it down. Be clear about how you are defining "wast-
ing time" because watching reality TV might be an essential
part of your relaxation strategy. Don't let other voices give you
the answer; define it for yourself.

CONSCIOUSLY CLARIFY
Shift into a Different Choice

Now that you've exposed your feelings and beliefs, go back to what you've written and use the questions here to respond to yourself from your most clear, wise, and loving place. Talk back to yourself. Let solutions and new choices emerge in response.

1. Though it is natural for me to fear losing certain abilities, traits, and other skills as I age, what are three valuable abilities, traits, or skills I now have as a result of age that I did not have ten, fifteen, or twenty years ago?

2. When I look back and identify the qualities I believe I
   don't have anymore, is there any way I can reclaim them
   in my life now, or must I bid farewell to that part of me
   and try to accept the losses with grace?

3. While I may have heard messages as a child that enticed me to believe I am not lovable or worthy of celebration, I now see where those voices originate, and how I've absorbed them as my own. What are the messages I can tell myself now that encourage me to consider the real possibility that I am indeed lovable and worthy of celebration?

4. What choices can I make to reclaim time in my life? How can I transform the habits that waste time and, instead, create new rituals and routines that are more nurturing and fulfilling to me?

5. Now that I have more clarity around why birthdays can be a challenge for me, what are three areas that excite me about celebrating my next birthday?

REMEMBER YOUR PURPOSE
Embrace the Reason You're Here

As your birthday approaches, turn inward to discover (if you don't already know) what your life purpose is. Typically, it's a simple statement like, "My purpose is to motivate and inspire people to make positive change." "My purpose is to create beauty." "My purpose is to provide a loving and stable home for my family."

Answer the following even if you feel as if you're just using your imagination. Write freely and let it flow.

1. What is your positive purpose in life?

2. What is the one action you have done, or can do, to make this world a better place?

3. Do you wish your life purpose were different from what you currently believe it to be? If so, what is this new purpose?

PREPARE FOR JOY
List Everything You Love

While we know the actions and items that make us happy, we don't usually list them. By taking time to write down everything we love, we allow ourselves to have new ideas about ways to generate joy on our birthday. Since birthdays are the one day a year we get to have it all, allowing ourselves to remember everything we love gives us a better chance of actually creating the birthday we want.

People in Your Life

1. List all the people who make you feel good—
   even if you rarely spend time with them.

2. List all the people you have fun with—
   even if you rarely spend time with them.

3. List all the people whose sense of humor you really enjoy.

4. List all the people you trust with your deepest feelings.

5. List all the people you know personally whom you really admire.

6. List all the people with whom you wish you could spend more time.

Animals in Your Life

1. List your favorite animals.

2. List two ways you can spend time with animals in your local region.

Favorite Food

1. List your three favorite restaurants.

2. List your three favorite foods.

3. List your two favorite birthday cake flavors.

4. List your three favorite desserts.

Pleasurable Activities

1. List three activities you enjoy doing alone.

2. List three activities you enjoy doing with others.

Outdoor Places

1. List your three favorite outdoor places in your local area or region.

Sightseeing

1. List three local sites that you've never visited but would like to see.

2. List two towns or sites you'd like to visit that are within a two-hour drive.

Spiritual Places

1. Where do you find spiritual uplift and renewal?
    List all those places.

2. Are there any spiritually intriguing places you'd like
    to visit?

3. Where is the calmest or most healing spot in your home,
    garden, or neighborhood?

Spiritual Tools

1. What is your favorite spiritually inspiring book?

2. What is your favorite spiritual tool *(angel cards, scripture, medicine cards, tarot cards, I Ching)*?

3. What is your favorite spiritual practice?

4. What spiritual leader, if any, inspires you the most?

Creative Pursuits

1. List your two favorite creative pursuits whether you think you're talented at them or not.

2. List one way you could be creative on your birthday that sounds pleasurable.

Honoring Your Body

1. List the three ways you make your body feel good.

2. List your favorite form of physical expression.

3. What do you love wearing the most that makes you feel wonderful?

What Makes You Feel Special

1. List two times in your life that you have felt the most special.

2. Can you imagine how that feeling might be generated on your birthday? If so, how?

3. List three kindnesses you can do for the person
    closest to you to make them feel special.

Even though this workbook is about you, thinking of others can
make it easier to think of yourself.

RISING TO THE TOP

Now that you've listed a variety of people, things, and activities, carefully review them and write down which ones rise to the top. Which of them excites you enough to include them in your birthday celebration?

CAST A SPELL
FOR THE COMING YEAR
Envision What You Want

As you ponder what you want to manifest in the coming year, think about what you deeply desire and imagine how you can bring it to life. Use the following as examples and then determine what you want to envision.

1. Do you desire more creative expression? If so, what does it look or sound or feel like? What can you do to manifest your creative desire? What promise can you make to yourself? By when will you start fulfilling this promise?

2. Do you desire more health in your life? If so, what specifically do you wish for? What can you do to begin manifesting your health in ways that are real and doable? What promise can you make to yourself? By when will you start fulfilling this promise?

3. Do you desire more abundance? Of what? Be specific
   and realistic. What can you do to begin manifesting
   abundance in ways that are real and doable? What
   promise can you make to yourself? By when will you start
   fulfilling this promise?

4. Do you desire more serenity? What do you really mean? What can you do to begin manifesting serenity in ways that are under your control? What promise can you make to yourself? By when will you start fulfilling this promise?

5. Do you desire more fun? What are the qualities that fun brings about in your life? How can you bring more fun into your life? What promise can you make to yourself? By when will you start fulfilling this promise?

DIAL IT IN

Pick the number-one wish you have for yourself that you'd like to manifest for the coming year, and write it down in current terms. For example, rather than saying something like, "With this personal new year, I will express my creative self and will finish writing my book," say, "With this personal new year, I am expressing my creative self and am finishing writing my book."

HAVE A HAPPY BIRTHDAY!

Acknowledgments

It took me a long time to write this book. Procrastination aside, I needed years to complete it because I had to live through many of my own birthdays while speaking with others about theirs. This enabled me to more deeply appreciate the range of expectations and emotions that so many of us have wrapped up in our birthdays, while at the same time confirming the transformative power that birthdays hold.

Only after hearing about and living through a wide range of experiences spanning more than two decades could I fully distill my perceptions into words. Most of this book was written in the days leading up to and immediately following my birthday. That's when my inspiration and clarity were at their peak.

I'd like to thank the early readers of my first draft—a vulnerable moment for writers. They were willing to test my advice as their birthdays approached and offered me real-time feedback and encouragement. Sparkling gratitude to Vernon Haney III, Ameet Kamath, Lori Leiter, Aleksandra Ponomareva, and Debbie Raphael. Vernon was especially transformed by my book and quoted lines from it to his family and friends. He kept asking when I was going to publish it, and his unwavering enthusiasm propelled me forward.

Thanks to other friends, family, and colleagues who gave me inspiration, feedback, and some gentle pushes: Cindy

Allsbrooks, Jennifer Ashby, Sue Artaud, Christa Assad, Lisa Awan, Josh Bazell, David Bedri, Jared Blumenfeld, Brittany Chan, Deborah Cooper, Xan Devaney, Josie Dominguez-Chand, Mira Dorrance-Bird, Sean Dorsey, Janelle Fitzpatrick, Bill Fleming, Lisa Fleming, Peter Gallotta, Todd Gelfand, Thea Hillman, Leo Hubbard, Faith Hurwitz, Ehulani Kane, Harold Linde, Jean Long, Marianne Manilov, Ilana McBride, Heather Persons, Rachel Pomerantz, Laurence Rosenthal, David Sobel, Jon Sorenson, Elizabeth Gelfand Stearns, and Johnny Wow.

Special thanks to Rae Dunn who cheered this project on for more than a decade, (after playing matchmaker for me and my husband, no less) and Rebecca Bazell who used her mighty red pen to edit my first draft and speak to me in that frank and humorous way only a good friend can. Arielle Eckstut came next with her insightful and professional developmental edit, and, after that, I had the wind at my back.

I'm grateful to the talented team of women who helped me move this book forward: Laura Duffy, Jenny Lisk, Karen Minster, Debra Nichols, Mary O'Donohue, and Sandra Wendel. Their involvement made me relax. And work hard.

Much love to my siblings Doreen Gelfand, Daniel Hurwitz, and Sharón Eliashar for their love and support, and for role modeling how to embrace life with adventure and joy. As young children, they all remember when I was born since they were raptly watching the *Wizard of Oz* that evening. This "origin story" that they often recounted wove colorful and mythic symbolism into my life while vividly anchoring me to the day of my birth.

When I look back on the early period of my truly happy birthdays, many of them included Tracy Dorrance who embraced her birthdays (and mine) with delight and majesty. She and I enthusiastically raised the birthday spirit together for years, and she deserves a mighty tip of the birthday crown from me. Thank you, Tracy!

I also want to acknowledge the brilliant Antero Alli, and all the years I studied with him. As my dear teacher, mentor, and friend, he taught me the power of thinking for yourself based on your lived experience. A man like that comes this way but once.

And finally, the most loving thanks of all goes to my wonderful husband, Drew Fleming. He inspired me to finally start writing this book and encouraged me by lighting up with joy each time I'd talk about my progress. Plus, he tirelessly helped me ideate, edit, and polish. The icing on the cake? He agreed that our next dog could be a toy poodle.

About the Author

Tamar Hurwitz-Fleming was born January 9, 1966, and grew up experiencing happy birthdays, disappointing birthdays, and downright terrible birthdays until she turned twenty and realized making her birthday happy was entirely up to her.

With each following year, Tamar started paying close attention to her energy as her birthday approached and how various factors—whether under her control or not—impacted her birthday experience. She noted those observations and put them to work in the following years, so that each January 9 thereafter she was able to successfully put herself at the center of her day and experience deep fulfillment.

She wrote this book to help people find deeper meaning and happiness on their birthdays too.

Tamar is an artist, astrologer, and award-winning environmental educator who has worked internationally and presented to more than 350,000 people, inspiring and motivating them to make positive behavior changes on behalf of the greater good. She and her husband, Drew, live in San Francisco and enjoy spending time in Santa Fe and Barcelona, where she became a Spanish citizen thanks to a law that welcomed the return of Sephardic Jews whose ancestors were expelled during the Spanish Inquisition of 1492. She is a big fan of tiny dogs and her favorite birthday cake is strawberry Chantilly.

Author's Note

If this book inspired you to approach your birthdays in a more creative, thoughtful, and positive manner, then my work is fulfilled and I am deeply gratified.

If you would like to gift this book to others, the ideal time to do so is four to six weeks before their birthday so they have enough time to read it, plan accordingly, and benefit from a happier birthday.

Thank you for sharing your time with me.